Jungle Beat

by Lynn Kleiner

ISBN 0-7390-3812-5 (Book and CD)

Alfred

Table of

Contents

Learning about the rainforest couldn't be more fun than through making music!

Inspiration and Gratitude

I want to thank the following friends and colleagues for their inspiration, support and ideas:

MISSY SIMPSON, *for your amazing décor and craft ideas and for always being so supportive of the Music Rhapsody program.*

UTE BRAUN, *yarn webs*

MARTIN ESPINO, *amazing instruments and awesome sounds!*

DENISE GAGNE, *balloon bat sounds*

BARBARA ANDRESS, *whom I've personally seen being swallowed by a Boa Constrictor!*

LESLIE ZEISS, *who added the jungle chant to the Jungle Beat song*

ANNA SONG, *Five Little Monkeys melody*

LILIAN YAROSS, *for inspiring us to prop up the day*

JEFF KRISKE *and* RANDY DELELLUS *for the spinning spider words and their example of striving to always be their best.*

Songs, Rhymes and Chants

Jungle Beat Chant  Track 1 & 30

Lynn Kleiner

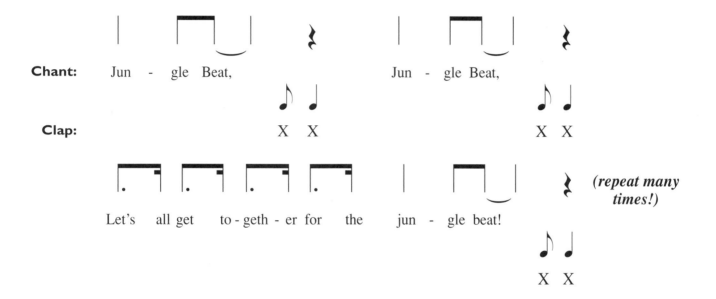

Chant: Jun - gle Beat,   Jun - gle Beat,

Clap: X X   X X

Let's all get to-geth-er for the   jun - gle beat!   *(repeat many times!)*

X X

SUGGESTIONS:

Movement
- Walk in place or around the room to the beat, chanting and clapping on the Xs.
- Walk to the beat, but stop on the Xs.

Body Sounds Track 3
- Listen to the chant with the students.
- Say the words and tap legs twice after saying the word "beat."
- Ask the students how they could make a sound with their body (clapping, patting, stamping, clicking the tongue, hitting the chest, etc.) after the word "beat."
- Encourage students to try their own ideas.
- Have students share their ideas with the class; repeat the chant using each other's ideas.
- Use vocal sounds to sound like a jungle bird, monkey, snake, etc. before and after saying the chant, and after the word "beat."

Percussion and Homemade Instruments
- Add percussion instruments, playing on the Xs after the word "beat."
- Have one kind of percussion (i.e., drums or rhythm sticks) play on the beat throughout the chant, while others (i.e., shakers or metals) play on the Xs.
- Use the rainstick for the introduction or throughout the chant.
- Use the jungle drum for scraping, shaking and other jungle sounds.

Orff Instruments Track 17
- Set up in F pentatonic (remove the B and E bars).
- Play any notes on the rests (Xs).
- On the lowest instruments, play D and A on the beat.

Jungle Music Track 2

Lynn Kleiner

The jungle can get so loud, you would want to cover your ears!
Larger animals have a low, loud voice.
The elephant uses sounds so low, people cannot hear them, and they make vibrating rumbles through the ground.
Of course, they also "trumpet!"
The small cricket has a very high-pitched voice.
Howler monkeys holler loud across the jungle!
Chimpanzees are jungle drummers!
They bang their feet and hands on buttress roots to make a bass drum sound
Bats squeak, and some kinds honk!
Frogs and toucans make a croacking sound,
And the animals make lots of noises as they move around,
and when they eat!

SUGGESTIONS:

Body Sounds
- Clapping, patting, stamping, clicking the tongue, or hitting the chest will add to the jungle sound!

Percussion and Homemade Instruments
- Use jungle drums, rhythm sticks, guiros, or homemade drums, shakers and rainsticks to create a jungle-like atmosphere!

We're Going to the Jungle Today!

Lynn Kleiner

Oh we're go - ing to the jun - gle to - day.___ *Oh yeah!* Oh we're

go - ing to the jun - gle to - day.___ *Oh yeah!* Keep the beat in your feet we're

in for a treat___ *Oh yeah!* in the jun - gle to - day.___ *Oh yeah so*

good! In the jun - gle to - day.___ *Oh yeah so good!* In the jun - gle to - day, *yeah!*

Verse 1: The snakes in the trees are hidden away,
Put hands together in front of body and move in snake-like motions, then hide hands behind back
The monkeys are out, 'cause they want to play!
Use arms for monkey gestures
The birds are flappin', let's play too!
Flap arms like a bird
They make such noise, cu-cu, cu-cu!
Make bird sounds in a high voice and other jungle sounds

Verse 2: Lots of fruit and lots of seeds
Plenty for all to munch and feed
Cocoa, chocolate, nuts and spice
Treats from the jungle, Mm-Mm, nice!

SUGGESTIONS:

Body Sounds

- Choose sounds such as clapping, patting, stamping, clicking the tongue, hitting the chest, or jungle sounds, such as monkeys, birds, etc. to be heard before and after the song and on the Xs (rests).
- Hand clap with a partner on the Xs.
- Stamp on the Xs and on the words "beat in your feet."

Percussion and Homemade Instruments

- Play in the same places as described above using found objects, homemade instruments, or percussion instruments such as drums, shakers, sticks, etc.

Orff Instruments

- Set up in F pentatonic (remove the B and E bars).
- Play any notes on the rests (Xs).
- On the lowest instruments, play D and A, or just the biggest D on the beat.

Sixty Inches of Rain Track 5

Lynn Kleiner

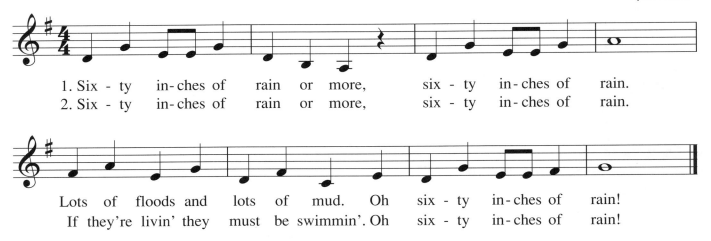

1. Six - ty   in - ches of   rain or more,   six - ty   in - ches of   rain.
2. Six - ty   in - ches of   rain or more,   six - ty   in - ches of   rain.

Lots of floods and   lots of mud. Oh   six - ty   in - ches of   rain!
If they're livin' they   must be swimmin'. Oh   six - ty   in - ches of   rain!

SUGGESTIONS:

Movement

- After singing Verse 1, have students sing the melody of the song using the syllable "ah," with heads tilted back and mouths open, as if they are catching rain drops.
- "Create Your Own Thunderstorm" can be performed after each verse for added effect.

Instruments

- Play rainsticks or other shakers throughout the song.

Create Your Own Thunderstorm Track 6

SUGGESTIONS:

This piece uses body sounds to mimic the sounds of a thunderstorm, and moves from soft to loud, then back to soft.

Movement

- Students sit in a circle, with the teacher or a designated student as the leader.
- Without speaking, the leader will begin playing. The student to the right of the leader will begin next, and so on, around the circle.
- Once everyone is playing, the leader decides when to move on to the next sound, and does so again without speaking.
- The student to the right of the leader should always be watching and listening for cues to move on to the next sound.
- Once everyone is stamping their feet, the leader should begin repeating the steps in backwards order, so that the storm "quiets."

Body Sounds

- Quickly rub the palms of hands together.
- Use two fingers of one hand to tap (clap) on the other hand.
- Use four fingers of one hand to tap (clap) on the other hand.
- Clap hands together.
- Quickly pat hands on legs.
- Stamp feet.

Going to the Jungle, Sing What We Should Bring Track 7

Lynn Kleiner

Swing it!

Go - ing   to   the   jun - gle   X   Don't for - get   a   thing   X   Sa -

far - i   time   is   here   now   X   Sing   what   we   should   bring.   X
Last time: That's   what   we   will   bring.   *Yeah!*

(repeat ad lib. from beginning)

solo   *echo*

We should bring   bi - no - cu - lars.   We should bring   bi - no - cu - lars.

Going to the Jungle (hit), Don't forget a thing (hit),
Safari time is here now (hit), Sing what we should bring (hit).
We should bring (a) _____.
(Use your jungle cards for examples, or make up your own supplies!)
We should bring (a) _____.

SUGGESTIONS:
- Use the jungle drum to play the (hit).
- The person playing the drum can sing the solo.
- For a large class, pass the drum during the song, letting students make up items before singing the entire song again. After four or five people, go back to the beginning.

Visuals
- **To make Jungle Cards, copy the pictures on page 61 and follow these instructions:**
  1. Cut out, glue felt to the back of the pictures.
  2. Have each child select a picture to use for the song.
  3. After the soloist names their supply, all other children echo in response.
  4. After singing, the soloist places the card on the felt board.
  5. Repeat, until all the cards have been used.

Jungle Beat Track 8

Valerie Johnson
Arr. Lynn Kleiner

Two lit-tle mon-keys sil-ly and neat___ said, "Let's find the jun-gle beat."___ They found some sticks and they tapped the ground and said, "Hey! That's a migh-ty cool sound!"

Verse 2:   Two little monkeys, silly and neat,
Said, "Let's find the jungle beat."
They found some skins and they tapped 'em with their hands
And said, "Hey! That's a mighty cool band."

Verse 3:   Two little monkeys, silly and neat,
Said, "Let's find the jungle beat."
They found some metals that were left by a king
And said, "Hey! That's a mighty cool ring."

Verse 4:   All the little monkeys at the end of the week,
Get together for the jungle beat.
They play all the instruments that they have found
And say, "Hey! That's the coolest sound around."

SUGGESTIONS:

Percussion and Homemade Instruments
- Play instruments twice after the word "Hey!" then "free" play after the verse is sung.
- Use the jungle drum to play on the two beats following "Hey!"
- Verse 1- Play sticks, such as rhythm sticks, chop sticks, lummi sticks, and unsharpened pencils.
- Verse 2- Play skins, such as hand drums, tambourines homemade jungle drums or empty water cooler jugs.
- Verse 3- Play metals, such as finger cymbals, triangles, key rings full of keys, chimes, pots and pans.
- Verse 4- Play all of the above!
- **See page 43 for instructions on how to make a homemade Jungle Drum!**

Orff Instruments
- Set up instruments in G pentatonic by removing the C and F bars.
- The steady beat can be played on the biggest E and B.
- Have children play any two notes twice after the word "Hey!"
- Children may make up their own jungle beat song after the verse is sung, using any notes.

Five Little Monkeys Track 9

Leader: *How many monkeys?* **Group:** *One, two, three, four, five!*

Arr. Lynn Kleiner
Inspired by Anna Song

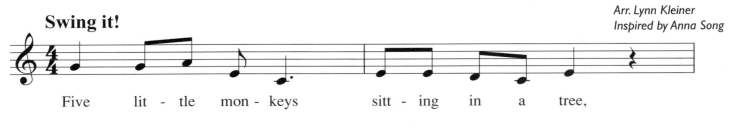

Five lit - tle mon - keys sitt - ing in a tree,

teas - in' mis - ter croc - o - dile you can't catch me.

(Speak, starting soft and getting louder) Along comes Mister Crocodile...and, SNAP!

Leader: *How many monkeys?* **Group:** *One, two, three, four!*
(Repeat verse with "four" little monkeys)

After "one", the teacher says "Wait, look! The monkeys were just hiding! They laugh, they high-five, then they swing in the trees to tease poor Mr. Crocodile some more."

SUGGESTIONS:

Counting Monkeys Before Each Verse
- Any of the sounds listed below can be played while counting monkeys, before each verse is sung.
- **See page 47 for an accompanying craft that students will love to use with this song!**

Body Sounds
- Pat thighs on a steady beat while singing the song.
- Pat beat on thighs, adding a clap after singing "tree" and "me."
- Find a partner and sing the song while keeping the beat on the thighs, but clap with the partner after singing "tree" and "me."
- Perform the crescendo by patting quickly (tremolo) on their legs.

Percussion Instruments
- Use the jungle drum and play the crescendo (going from soft to loud) as everyone says "Along comes Mister Crocodile!" and hit once on "Snap!"
- Use rhythm sticks to keep the beat on the floor during the song, hitting the sticks together after "tree" and "me."
- During "Along comes Mister Crocodile!" rub rhythm sticks together, starting slow and soft, growing to fast and loud, then hit together on "Snap!"
- To play hand drums, have two children sit across from each other with the instrument between them on the floor.
- Each student keeps the beat on the drum during the song and claps with their partner after "tree" and "me."
- Crescendo (play from soft to loud) on the drum during "Along comes Mister Crocodile!"
- Each student taps their partner's hands on "Snap!"

Orff Instruments
- Set up instruments in C pentatonic by removing the F and B bars.
- Low instruments play the steady beat on the biggest C and G, and high instruments play after the words "tree" and "me" on any pentatonic notes during the song.
- During "Along comes Mister Crocodile!" all instruments alternate quick strokes between any two notes (tremolo) and crescendo (soft to loud). Click mallets together on "Snap!"

Introducing Music Vocabulary:
Tremolo (rapid repetition)
Crescendo (to grow from soft to loud)
Piano (soft)
Forte (loud)

The Spider Kept on Spinning

Lynn Kleiner

The spi-der kept on spin-ning. The spi-der kept on spin-ning. The

spi-der kept on spin-ning un-til his work was done.

(Speak)

In the Jungle, the monkeys are using their tails to help them balance and swing from tree to tree.
While...
(Verse)
The spider kept on spinning, the spider kept on spinning,
The spider kept on spinning, until his work was done.

The crocodile lies with his mouth open and allows the birds to safely pick food from his teeth.
While...
(Repeat Verse)

The python, a very choosy eater, watches what he wants to eat for days. He swallows his food
whole, and especially likes lizards for his lunch.
And all the while...
(Repeat Verse)

The tree frog uses his sticky toes to help him hold on to the branches.
While...
(Repeat Verse)

The butterflies fly together in large groups. Many butterflies can taste with their feet!
While...
(Repeat Verse)

The sloths are the slowest mammal on the earth. Sloths live in trees and spend almost all of their
time hanging upside down from tree branches!
But...
(Repeat Verse)

Finally, the spider rested and watched as bugs became caught in his web.

SUGGESTIONS:

Yarn Spider Web
- Have children sit in a circle, with one child holding a ball of yarn.
- While holding the loose end of the yarn, the child should roll the ball across the circle to another classmate, so that there is a line of yarn between them.
- Repeat four times, once during each line: "the spider kept on spinning" and "until his work was done."
- The yarn should be rolled to a different person each time, so that an intricate "web" is formed.
- It is important to remind the children to hold the loose end of the yarn in one hand as they pass the ball.
- Continue passing every time the verse is sung.

Movement
- Have some children spin and dance outside of the web circle while holding black scarves or streamers.
- When the web is complete, children throw their scarves and streamers into the web to be "caught."

A Classroom Caught in a Web
- Give each child a small ball of yarn.
- During the verse, have children wind their yarn around the room, wrapping it around chairs, table legs, etc., making a web.
- After the song, have children try to walk through their webs.

Percussion Instruments
- Use drums and hand percussion instruments to create a jungle-like atmosphere during the spoken parts.
- Play finger cymbals or triangles after "spinning" and "done."

Orff Instruments
- Low instruments: Play the steady beat throughout the song on the biggest E, or play the biggest E and B together. To make playing easier, remove bars that are not played.
- Middle instruments: Drag a mallet up and down a complete set of bars without picking it up (glissandos) throughout the song.
- High instruments: Set up instruments in G pentatonic by removing the C and F bars. Play any pentatonic notes (E, G, A, B or D) after "spinning" (3 times) and "done."
- **See page 49 for an accompanying craft that children will love to use with this song!**

Two Talking Toucans

arr. Lynn Kleiner

Two talk - ing tou - cans sitt - ing in a tree. Two talk - ing tou - cans sitt - ing in a tree.

Call: What happened? **Response:** One flew away! *(Play instruments as one flies away)*

Verse 2: One talking toucan, sitting in a tree, *(Repeat)*

Call: What happened? **Response:** One flew away! *(Play instruments as one flies away)*

Verse 3: No talking toucans, sitting in a tree, *(Repeat)*

Call: What happened? **Response:** One flew back! *(Play instruments as one flies back)*

Verse 4: One talking toucan, sitting in a tree, *(Repeat)*

Call: What happened? **Response:** One flew back! *(Play instruments as one flies back)*

Verse 5: Two talking toucans, sitting in a tree, *(Repeat)*

SUGGESTIONS:

Movement
- Divide children into partners, and give each two scarves or feathers to hold.
- After singing Verse 1, one partner "flies away" to another point in the room.
- After singing Verse 2, the second partner "flies" to join the first.
- After singing Verse 3, the first partner "flies" back to the starting place, their "tree."
- After singing Verse 4, the second partner "flies" back to join the first.

Orff Instruments
- Set up instruments in C pentatonic by removing the F and B bars.
- During verses, have low instruments play a steady beat on the biggest C and G bars.
- While a toucan is "flying," use hands to play any notes on middle and high instruments. Stop playing when the toucan has "landed."
- Assign different instruments to play for specific toucans, or have all instruments play whenever any toucan is flying.

Percussion Instruments

- Hand percussion, such as wood blocks, bells, or triangles can be selected by the players to accompany the toucans who "fly away" and return.

- Assign different instruments to play for specific toucans, or have all instruments play whenever any toucan is flying.

- **See page 52 for an accompanying craft that children will love to use with this song!** Have each child create two homemade toucans, one for each hand. Sing the song as written, and have the children hide a toucan behind their back when it "flies away."

Toucan Facts to Share

Toucans like to be with their toucan friends; when they are, they are quite a noisy bunch!

Toucans look for existing holes in trees to make their homes and lay eggs.

When toucans eat fruit, they eat it whole and then throw up the seeds. (This is helpful in the jungle for growing more fruit trees!)

Bats

Jungle, Jungle,
Bats all a-flutter,
They're really very harmless, but it
Makes my body shudder!

*Quickly shake balloon back and forth (right to left),
so the balloon hits the sides of the hand.*

Jungle, Jungle,
Quick bats fly,
Listen to their squeaky sound,
Listen to them cry.

*Place the round part of the balloon against
bellybutton with opening facing out.*

*Make squeaky sounds with the balloon by
pulling the opening tight.*

Jungle, Jungle,
Quick bats fly,
Down to the jungle floor,
Up to the sky!

*Quickly shake balloon back and forth (right to left),
so the balloon hits the sides of the hand.*

Let the balloons go to see the "quick bats fly!"

SUGGESTIONS:

Movement
- Let children move high, low and around the room very quickly.
- Encourage children to use their excellent bat radar so they don't bump anyone or anything!
- **See page 50 for an accompanying craft that children will love to use with this song!**

Balloons
- Blow up a small balloon for each child, but do not tie it in a knot.
- Perform the above gestures in correspondence with the lyrics.

I'm Being Swallowed by a Boa Constrictor

Shel Silverstein
Arr. Lynn Kleiner

SUGGESTIONS:

Movement
- Encourage the children to point to their toes, knees, thighs, middle, and neck as they are singing, in the order that they are being "swallowed."
- Have children sing the A Section at the end of the song with the mouth closed and arms hugging body, as if being muffled by being inside the boa constrictor.
- Children can also use sleeping bags to pull up around them, or stretchy, snakeskin-like fabrics. Pull the bag or fabric up to each body part as it is named in the song.

Orff Instruments
- In the B Section, start on C and play four steady beats for one measure, then move to the next note. Play four beats on each bar up to G, then play A, B, and high C for one beat each.

Silly Sam  Track 14

Lynn Kleiner

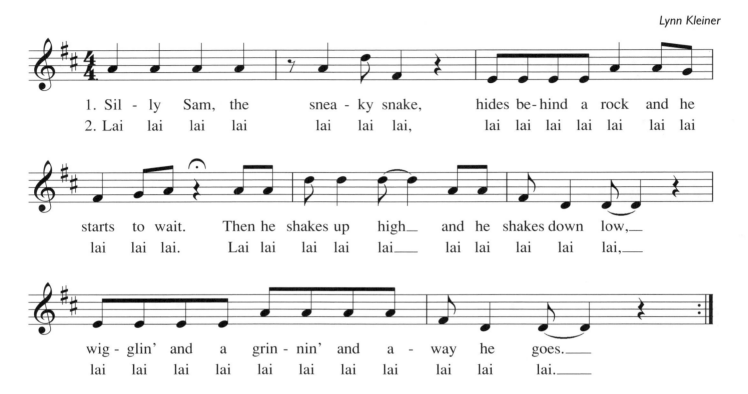

1. Sil - ly Sam, the snea - ky snake, hides be-hind a rock and he
2. Lai lai lai lai lai lai lai, lai lai lai lai lai lai lai

starts to wait. Then he shakes up high___ and he shakes down low,___
lai lai lai. Lai lai lai lai lai___ lai lai lai lai lai,___

wig - glin' and a grin - nin' and a - way he goes.___
lai lai lai lai lai lai lai lai lai lai lai.___

SUGGESTIONS:

Movement
- Dance with shakers throughout the song.
- Have children hide the shakers behind their backs after the word "wait."
- Play shakers high above head and low to the ground when indicated in the song.
- **See page 46 to learn how to make a Rattlin' Sock Snake and a shaker egg!**

Follow the Leader Game
- Once the children know how to sing the song without the CD, use one snake puppet and choose one child to be "Silly Sam," the leader.
- After singing the word "wait," the leader hides the snake behind their back, and all other children follow with their shakers.
- The leader decides how long the silence will be.
- Before the verse is sung again, the leader gives the snake to another child, who becomes the new leader.

Listening for the Letter S!

Make up a story using words that start with the letter 'S,' or use the story below. Have children shake their shaker snake when they hear an 'S' word!

Story

Silly Sam, the sneaky snake, slithered slowly out from under the rock. Silly Sam stopped suddenly when he thought he saw his supper. "Super, supper," he said when he saw the sleepy crocodile swimming slowly in the swamp. Silly Sam stared at the slow swimmer who stopped, then sank. Still searching for his supper, Silly Sam slipped away.

Up So High

Lynn Kleiner

Up so high, down so low. Give a lit-tle shake and a-round we go.

Up so high, down so low. Give a lit-tle shake, now hold them so.

SUGGESTIONS:

Movement
- Follow the words of the song for movement directions.
- Have children mimic the teacher's "freeze" position when the word "so" is sung (ex. hold shaker on head, foot, behind back, elbow, etc.).
- Assign a child to be the leader who decides where to put the shaker on the last "freeze."

Homemade Instruments
- **See page 46 for instructions on how to make a Rattlin' Sock Snake and a shaker egg!**

Now My Shaker's Up/Where Are You?

Track 16

Arr. Lynn Kleiner

Now my sha - ker's up and now my sha - ker's down. Now my sha - ker's

dan - cing all a - round the town. Dance it by your shoul - der,

dance it by your head. Dance it by your knees, now tuck it in - to bed.

Sha - ker, sha - ker, where are you?

Here I am, here I am, how do you do?!

SUGGESTIONS:

Movement

- Perform the two songs back to back, with or without pause.
- Use a shaker throughout the performance.
- Follow directions for movement provided by the words of the song.
- On the last line, "tuck it into bed", cross arms to hide hands and shaker. Keep the shaker hidden until "Here I am" is sung in "Where Are You?".

Homemade Instruments

- **See page 46 for instructions on how to make a shaker egg to use with this song!**

The Butterfly Track 18

Traditional
Arr. Lynn Kleiner

Way up in the skies, a butterfly flies.
When way down below, a caterpillar goes slow.
He munches and munches on jungle leaf lunches.
"I'm so full and fat," he says with a pat.
"I'll spin a cocoon by the light of the moon,
Curl into my bed and sleep," he said.
Not a sound did we hear, till the special moment was near.
The weeks soon passed by, and out flew a butterfly!

SUGGESTIONS:

Movement
- Give each child a brightly colored scarf to use.
- Use these gestures to correspond to the following speaking parts:

Way up in the skies, a butterfly flies.
For one scarf, hold in the middle and move hand up and down to create wings; for two scarves, hold one in each hand and flap "wings" to mimic a butterfly.

When way down below, a caterpillar goes slow.
Crawl, belly down, slowly on the floor.

He munches and munches on jungle leaf lunches.
Move mouth in vigorous chewing movements.

"I'm so full and fat," he says with a pat.
Pat belly.

"I'll spin a cocoon by the light of the moon,
Spin around with scarves in hand.

Curl into my bed and sleep," he said.
Wrap scarf around your head and lay down.

Not a sound did we hear, till the special moment was near.
Lay still.

The weeks soon passed by, and out flew a butterfly!
"Fly" around with scarves in hand, creating "wings" again.

Orff and Percussion Instruments

- Set up instruments in a pentatonic scale. For example, in C pentatonic, remove the F and B bars.
- Improvise on instruments to create sound effects that correspond to the speaking parts.

Way up in the skies, a butterfly flies.
Play any combination of notes in quick patterns on the highest instruments (remind children that the highest instruments have the smallest or shortest bars).

When way down below, a caterpillar goes slow.
Play any combination notes in slow patterns on the low instruments (remind children that the lowest instruments have the biggest or longest bars).

He munches and munches on jungle leaf lunches.
Ribbed tone blocks, guiros, or even the ribs of a plastic "to go" food container played with a chop stick will work for chewing sounds!

"I'm so full and fat," he says with a pat.
Roto-toms work great for an "indigestion" sound, going from low to high as the drum is turned; kids also like to burp!

"I'll spin a cocoon by the light of the moon,
Play glissandos up and down middle instruments with all bars in place.

Curl into my bed and sleep," he said.
Play softly on triangles and finger cymbals.

Not a sound did we hear, 'til the special moment was near.
Silence!

The weeks soon passed by, and out flew a butterfly!
Play any combination of notes in quick patterns on the highest instruments.

Visuals

- **See page 51 for an accompanying craft that children will love to use with this song!**

"Grr-umph!" Went the Little Green Frog

Traditional
Arr. Lynn Kleiner

SUGGESTIONS:

Body Sounds

- Ask children to suggest different sounds for the words "Grr-umph!", "bloop, bloop, bloop" and "La-di-da-di-da."

Percussion Instruments

- Rub a mallet across a ribbed tone block for "grr-umph!," hit the block with a mallet for "bloop, bloop, bloop," and put the mallet inside the block and gently shake it back and forth for "La-di-da-di-da."
- Drag a chop stick or mallet along the ribbed side of a homemade jungle drum for "grr-umph!," hit the top like a drum for "bloop, bloop, bloop," and use as a shaker for "La-di-da-di-da."
- **See page 43 for instructions on how to make a homemade Jungle Drum!**

 GRR-UMPH

Ten Little Froggies

Arr. Lynn Kleiner

One lit-tle frog-gie goes— hop. One! A - long comes a-noth-er and they just can't stop! Two lit-tle frog-gies go— hop. One, two! A - long comes a-noth-er and they just can't stop! Three lit-tle frog-gies go—

(continue adding froggies until...)

hop. *One, two, three.* A - long comes a-noth-er and they just can't stop!

Ten lit-tle frog-gies go— hop! *One, two three, four, five, six, seven, eight, nine, ten.* DROP! TIME TO STOP!

One little froggie goes hop, *(count: "one")*
Along comes another and they just can't stop, oh...
Two little froggies go hop, *(count: "one, two")*
Along comes another and they just can't stop, oh...
Three little froggies go hop, *(count: "one, two, three")*
Along comes another and they just can't stop, oh...
Continue adding froggies until...
Ten little froggies go hop, *(count: "one, two, three, four, five, six, seven, eight, nine, ten")*
(Speak) "Drop! Time to stop!"

SUGGESTIONS:

Movement
- Count as many frogs as there are children.
- Assign each child a specific number.
- When a child is added, they may "hop" only when they are counting their number. Younger children enjoy jumping during their entire verse and thereafter.
- When everyone has counted, the teacher speaks the last line "Drop! Time to stop!" so children fall and freeze.

Percussion Instruments
- Have hand drums or homemade drums play a steady beat throughout the song, until the word "stop."
- Have smaller instruments, such as woodblocks or sticks, play on the numbers.

Orff Instruments
- Set up the instruments in G pentatonic by removing the C and F bars.
- Have low instruments play a 4-beat introduction before the singing begins on each verse, and then a steady beat on big E and B bars until the word "stop."
- On each spoken number, play any notes on middle and high instruments using both hands.
- For an additional challenge, have bars set up on B, A, G, F#, E, D, E and play a descending scale on "along comes another and they just can't stop."

Visuals
- Cut frog patterns (p. 57) out of paper or felt and use to illustrate this song.
- **See page 53 for another accompanying craft that children will love to use with this song!**

A Salamander Track 21

Traditional

I saw a little creature that was slimy, smooth, and wet.
I thought it was the oddest thing that I had ever met.
It was something like a lizard, but it had no scales at all.
It was something like a frog, but it didn't hop—it crawled.
So I took it to my teacher, and she told me right away,
"I see you brought a salamander into class today."

SUGGESTIONS:

Percussion Instruments

- Choose any type of percussion instrument to play on rhyming words at the end of each line.
- Select other words to play on with different instruments, such as "lizard," "frog," "teacher," or "salamander."
- Try playing a different instrument on the last three beats of each line.

Matilda the Gorilla

Track 22

Not too Fast

mf

Mary Rice Hopkins

1. In the jun-gle I___ saw a go-ril-a, and
2. Ma-til-da is as ha-py as can be. She

her name, she was a Ma-til-da. Ma-til-da loved to sing songs
eats her ba-nan-nas and swings from the trees. Now with her friends___

ev-er-y day and this is what Ma-til-da the go-ril-la would say. "Ah-
you will see, the sing-ing Ma-til-da__ fam-i-ly.__

ooh, ooh, ooh, ooh, ah, ah, ah,___ ah-ooh, ooh, ooh, ooh,

ah, ah, ah,___ ah-ooh, ooh, ooh, ooh,

ah, ah, ah,___ ooh-ooh-ah ooh, ooh, ah-ah, ah!"___

SUGGESTIONS:

Movement

- Ask for volunteers to participate in the movements.
- During the verse, have students perform simple steps in rhythm, such as clapping, snapping fingers, or stepping in line.
- Switch movements for every verse.
- During the chorus, have students perform monkey-like gestures in rhythm; bow down low with hands under arms for "ooh-ooh-ooh-ooh" and wave arms above head for "ah-ah-ah," just like a gorilla!

Notes:

The Elephant  Track 23

Traditional

The elephant goes like this and that,
(Sway side to side.)
He's terribly big and he's terribly fat!
(Put arms straight up in the air, then straight out from side.)
He has no fingers, he has no toes,
(Clench hands in a fist, then point to toes.)
But goodness gracious, what a nose!
(Put hands on hips, then make a "trunk" with arm.)

SUGGESTIONS:

Elephant Trunk
Use your elephant puppet (item #23839, included in the deluxe kit, item #23837):

- Encourage the children to make the elephant's trunk go up by making their voices higher.
- When voices go up, the trunk should rise up.
- When voices slide down, the trunk should respond by sliding down also.
- Encourage children to move their voices up, down and all around and watch the trunk follow!
- This activity is not only fun for the children, it will also help to increase their vocal range as they explore high and low sounds with their voices.

One Little Elephant 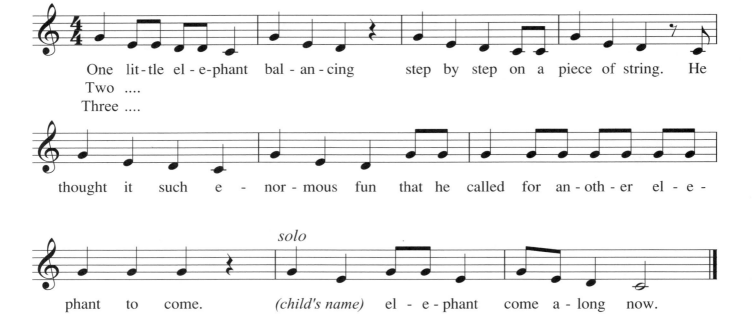 Track 24

One lit-tle el-e-phant bal-an-cing step by step on a piece of string. He
Two ....
Three ....

thought it such e-nor-mous fun that he called for an-oth-er el-e-

solo

phant to come. *(child's name)* el-e-phant come a-long now.

All the little elephants balancing,
Step by step on a piece of string!
They thought it was such enormous fun,
'Til the piece of string broke... *(Pause)* **Crash!** *(All fall down!)*
Then there were none!
Teacher solo: "Yoo hoo, elephants, your fun is done!"

SUGGESTIONS:

Movement

- Place a long piece of string on the floor, forming a large circle.
- Have children sit in a line on one side of the room.
- One child holds the elephant puppet and pretends to be "balancing" as they walk on the string.
- At the end of the song, the child sings the name of the next "elephant," passes the puppet to the new leader, and follows behind them.

Orff and Percussion Instruments

- Every child has an instrument at the beginning of the song except the first to "balance" on the string with the elephant puppet (item #23839, included in the deluxe kit, item #23837).
- Set up Orff instruments in C pentatonic by removing the B and E bars.
- Instruments such as triangles, finger cymbals, drums, high Orff instruments, or others selected by the children can play on the rests, or every eighth beat, which is usually a rest. There are also Xs in the music that indicate where to play.
- Lower Orff instruments play a steady beat during the song.
- The beat can be played on C and G, or from low G to high G throughout the song.

Five Little Speckled Frogs Track 25

Lively!

Virginia Pavelko / Lucille Wood
Arr. Lynn Kleiner

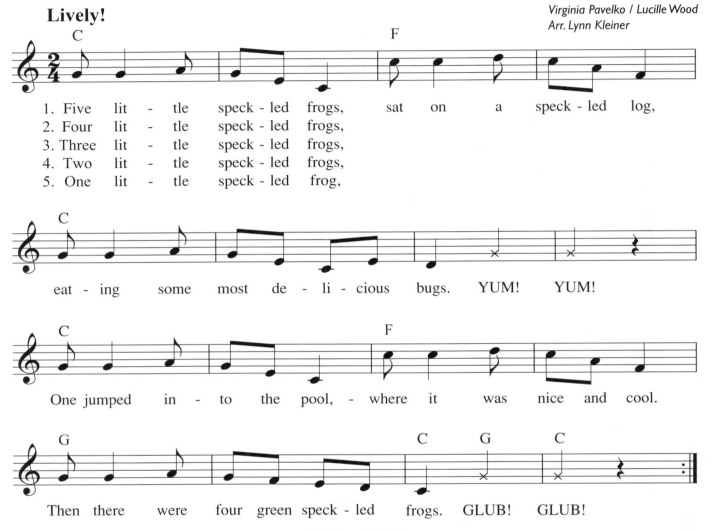

1. Five lit - tle speck - led frogs, sat on a speck - led log,
2. Four lit - tle speck - led frogs,
3. Three lit - tle speck - led frogs,
4. Two lit - tle speck - led frogs,
5. One lit - tle speck - led frog,

eat - ing some most de - li - cious bugs. YUM! YUM!

One jumped in - to the pool, - where it was nice and cool.

Then there were four green speck - led frogs. GLUB! GLUB!

SUGGESTIONS:

Percussion Instruments
- Have some children keep the beat on the song using ribbed rhythm sticks or guiro tone blocks, scraping them together for "yum, yum."
- Have children choose a variety of instruments to play on the word "jump."

Visuals
- Cut frog patterns (pp. 62-63) out of paper or felt and use to illustrate the disappearing frogs.
- **See page 53 for an accompanying craft that children will love to use with this song!**

Walking Through the Jungle, What Do You See? Track 26

Arr. Lynn Kleiner

Walk - in' through the jun - gle, what do you see?

I see a _____ look - ing at me.

SUGGESTIONS:

Percussion Instruments
- The child with the jungle drum plays a steady beat throughout the song, and sings the solo at the end.
- Ideas for items to sing can be taken from the images on the jungle drum or jungle cards.

Visuals
- **To make Jungle Cards, copy the pictures on page 60 and follow these instructions:**
    1. Cut out, glue felt to the back of the pictures.
    2. Have each child select a picture to use for the song.
    3. After all the children sing the question together, individuals take turns and sing their solo response.
    4. After singing, the soloist places the card on the felt board.
    5. Repeat, until all the cards have been used.

Guantanamera Track 27

Hey, everyone!
It's time for a jungle party!
Bugs and bats! Butterflies and birds!
Lizards, snakes and monkeys can be heard!
Take a walk on the wild side. What do you see?
Show me your jungle moves, who will you be?

SUGGESTIONS:

Movement
- Encourage the children to move like jungle creatures.
- Stand in two long lines, which form "the alley."
- For older children and larger classes, have two children at one end of the lines move down the alley as jungle creatures.
- When they reach the opposite end, the next two children follow.
- For smaller classes, children can move like a jungle creature across the room one at a time.

Percussion Instruments
- Percussion instruments such as shakers, rhythm sticks, claves, etc. can be used as accompaniment.
- Homemade instruments may also be played.

Mister Sun

Track 28

Traditional

Oh Mis-ter Sun, Sun, Mis-ter Gold-en Sun, please shine down on___ me. Oh Mis-ter Sun, Sun, Mis-ter Gol-den Sun, hid-ing be-hind a tree. These lit-tle chil dren are___ ask-ing you to please come_ out so we can play with you. Oh Mis-ter Sun, Sun, Mis-ter Gold-en Sun, please shine down on___ me.

SUGGESTIONS:

Percussion Instruments
- Play triangles and finger cymbals after the word "sun."
- Have children hide their instruments behind their backs when singing "hiding behind a tree," and show them again on "please come out so we can play with you."

Orff instruments
- Set up instruments in G pentatonic by removing the C and F bars.
- Play any two notes after the word "sun" is sung.
- Improvise on metal instruments, such as glockenspiels and metallophones, after the song is sung.
- Have children hide their mallets behind their backs when singing "hiding behind a tree," and show them again when they sing "please come out so we can play with you."

The Lion Sleeps Tonight

Track 29

Arr. Paul Cummings
Words and Music by George David
Weiss, Hugo Peretti, and
Luigi Creatore

Wi-mo weh - a wi-mo weh - a   Wi-mo weh - a wi-mo weh - a   Wi-mo weh - a wi-mo weh - a

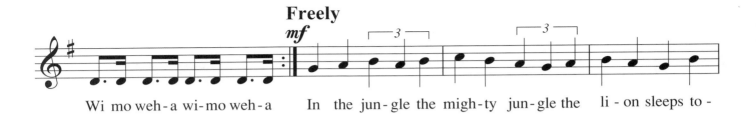

Freely
mf

Wi mo weh-a wi-mo weh-a   In the jun-gle the migh-ty jun-gle the   li - on sleeps to-

night!   In   the   jun - gle   the   migh - ty   jun - gle   the   li - on   sleeps   to-

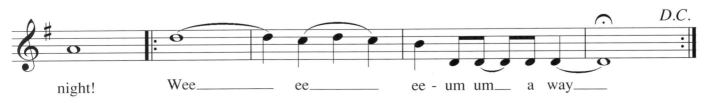

night!   Wee_____ ee_____   ee - um um___ a way___

Repeat several times and fade out to end.

SUGGESTIONS:

Percussion Instruments

- Choose a different percussion instrument for each section of the song; for instance, play rhythm sticks on part one, shakers on part two and hand drums during the verse.
- For older children, try singing and playing more than one section at the same time.

Jungle Instruments You Can Make

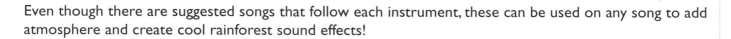

Even though there are suggested songs that follow each instrument, these can be used on any song to add atmosphere and create cool rainforest sound effects!

Jungle Drum

What You Need

Clear plastic "to go" food container with ribbed sides; can be round or square
Rice, beans, beads or pebbles (optional)
Colored paper
Paint and paint brush or markers
Double-sided tape
Chopstick or unsharpened pencil
Colorful electrical or masking tape
Scissors

What You Do

1. Trace the bottom of the container onto a piece of heavy paper and cut out the shape.
2. Paint or color a jungle picture or design on the paper.
3. Use double-sided tape to secure the paper to the bottom of the container.
4. Put a small amount of rice, beads or pebbles into the container to make an optional shaker.
5. Seal the container with electrical or masking tape.

How to Play

1. Using a chopstick or an unsharpened pencil, strike the top of the container for a drum sound, or scrape the ribbed sides for a guiro-like effect.
2. Move the container from side to side or up and down to create a shaker.

Use your new jungle drum with these fun songs!
"Jungle Beat Chant," p. 5
"We're Going to the Jungle Today!," p. 8
"Five Little Speckled Frogs," p. 38
"'Grr-umph!' Went the Little Green Frog," p. 28

Rainstick

What You Need
Paper towel tube
Aluminum foil
Glue
Tempera paints or markers
Paint brush
Colored electrical or masking tape
Rice
Yarn, construction paper or foam cut-outs, or other decorations
Scissors

What You Do
1. Make a construction paper cap and seal one end of the tube with tape, or fold one end of the tube over and staple it shut.
2. Make balls out of tin foil about the size of a golf ball or slightly smaller to fit in the tube.
3. Fill the tube with the foil balls up to an inch from the top.
4. Pour rice into the tube.
5. Seal or staple the other end of the tube.
6. Decorate by gluing yarn, construction paper, foam, or other decorations to the ends and sides of the tube.

How to Play
1. Tip the rain stick from side to side slowly, allowing the rice to "trickle" through the foil balls.
2. Experiment with the speed of the "tip" and see how many types of rainfall can be created.

Use your new rainstick with these fun songs!
"Jungle Beat Chant," p. 5
"Sixty Inches of Rain," p. 10
"The Lion Sleeps Tonight," p. 42

Jaguar Voice Rattle

What You Need
Paper towel tube
"Peanut-shaped" packing material
Orange tempera paint
Black tempera paint
Paint brush

What You Do
1. Paint the tube orange.
2. Dip the "peanuts" in a tray or plate of black paint.
3. Press the black "peanut" in different places on the orange tube to create "jaguar" spots.
4. Coat the tube with a non-toxic varnish (such as puzzle glue) once the tube is completely dry.

How to Play
1. Open mouth and tighten throat to make sound through the tube.
2. While "growling," stick lips out and form mouth into the word "wow."

Use your new jaguar voice rattle with these fun songs!
"Jungle Beat Chant," p. 5
"Jungle Music," p. 7
"Walking Through the Jungle, What Do You See?" p. 39

Rattlin' Sock Snake with Egg Shaker

What You Need
One tube sock
Markers, fabric, yarn or buttons
Plastic "fillable" egg
Rice
Colored electrical or masking tape

What You Do
1. Fill plastic egg with two teaspoons of rice.
2. Use tape to seal the egg shut.
3. Decorate the sock with eyes, nose (add mouth and tongue if desired).
4. Suggestions: Have the child hold onto the shaker while putting the sock on arm for an active rattling snake.

Try out your Rattlin' Sock Snake in "Silly Sam" on page 22!

Jungle Arts and Crafts

Clothes Pin Crocodile and Branch with Monkeys

What You Need

Clothes pin
Green tempera paint
Paint brush
Crocodile pattern (included on p. 58)
Green construction paper
Plastic "wiggly eyes"
Paper clips
Black permanent marker
Five different colors of construction paper
Brown construction paper
Self adhesive nylon fastening dots
Scissors

What You Do

1. Paint the clothes pin with green tempera paint.
2. Trace the crocodile pattern onto green construction paper.
3. Fold the paper in half and cut out the pattern.
4. Glue the flat side of the clothes pin to the bottom portion of the crocodile so that the opening of the clothes pin points toward the mouth.
5. Glue the top portion of the crocodile pattern to the bottom portion, enclosing the clothes pin.
6. Use paper clips to keep edges together until they dry. Remove paper clips.
7. Cut out a tree branch from brown construction paper.
8. Cut out monkeys from different colors of construction paper.
9. Attach one side of the nylon fastening dots to the monkeys, and the other to the branch.
10. Open the crocodile's mouth by squeezing its center, and place on monkey.

Paper Plate Snakes

What You Need
Paper plate
Scissors
Liquid water color paints
Paint brush
Plastic "wiggly eyes"
Red yarn, curling ribbon or paper
Glue

What You Do
1. Paint both sides of the paper plate and allow them to dry completely.
2. Start at the outer edge of the plate and cut in a spiral pattern towards the center.
3. Stop cutting about 4" from the center (the snake's head is the center of the plate).
4. Glue wiggly eyes to the head.
5. Glue red yarn or red curly ribbon in place for a tongue.

Spiders

What You Need

Foam insulated cups
Black permanent marker
Two pipe cleaners
Plastic "wiggly eyes"
Sharpened pencil
String or yarn
Cookie sheet
Oven (for adult use ONLY!)
Scissors

What You Do

1. Preheat oven to 350 degrees Fahrenheit.
2. Use a black marker to color the outside of the foam cup.
3. Using the pencil, push a piece of string through the top of the cup. Tie a knot inside the cup so the string cannot slip through.
4. Cut the pipe cleaners into four equal-length pieces.
5. Push the pipe cleaners into the bottom rim of the cup so that there are four on each side.
6. Place cups on a cookie sheet and bake for 2-3 minutes, or until shrunken.
7. Remove from oven and cookie sheet immediately and set on cooling rack.
8. When cool, glue on wiggly eyes.

Bats

What You Need

Foam insulated cups
Black permanent marker
Bat wing pattern (included on p. 59)
Black construction paper
Razor blade or knife (for adult use ONLY!)
Plastic "wiggly eyes"
Pencil or needle
String or yarn
Cookie sheet
Oven (for adult use ONLY!)

What You Do

1. Preheat oven to 350 degrees Fahrenheit.
2. Use a black marker to color the outside of the foam cup.
3. Using the pencil, push a piece of string through the top of the cup. Tie a knot inside the cup so the string cannot slip through.
4. Using a razor blade, CAREFULLY make a small slit on each side of the cup, just above the rim.
5. Trace two bat wings from the pattern onto black construction paper, and cut out.
6. Push each wing though a slit.
7. Place the cup on a cookie sheet and bake for 2-3 minutes, or until shrunken.
8. Remove from oven and cookie sheet immediately and set on cooling rack.
9. When cool, glue on wiggly eyes.

Butterfly

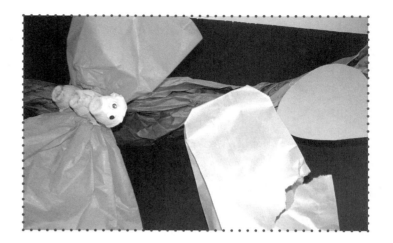

What You Need

*Colored tissue paper or white tissue paper painted
with watercolors*
Cardboard egg carton
Brightly colored tempera paint
Razor blade or knife (for adult use ONLY!)
Yarn
Glue, pipe cleaner or stapler
Plastic "wiggly eyes"
Small brown paper bag
Scissors

What You Do

1.   Cut the egg carton so that three egg holders remain attached to each other.
2.   Paint the egg holders in bright colors and let dry.
3.   Glue wiggly eyes on one end of the holder.
4.   Using the razor blade or knife, CAREFULLY poke a hole in the same end, and loop a piece of yarn through it. This is so the butterfly can hang from the ceiling or be "flown" by the child.
5.   Fold a piece of tissue paper to resemble a butterfly's wings.
6.   Attach the wings to the butterfly's body with glue, a pipe cleaner, or staples.
7.   Place the butterfly in a brown paper bag (its "cocoon").
8.   To surprise the children, take all the butterflies out of their cocoons one morning before class starts. Tear the bags so that it looks like the butterflies worked their way out!

Use this craft with the "The Butterfly" poem, p. 26!

Paper Plate Toucan

What You Need

Regular sized paper plate
Smaller sized paper plate
Tempera paint, markers or crayons in black, yellow, orange and red
Black construction paper
Hot glue gun
Stapler
Black feathers, tissue paper (optional)
Hole punch
Yarn
Scissors

What You Do

1. Paint or color the bottom or both sides of the larger paper plate black, leaving some white on one side for the "neck."
2. Paint or color the smaller paper plate (the "beak") in yellow, orange, and red and let dry (painting in stripes is suggested, but not necessary).
3. Fold both plates in half.
4. Glue the bottom of the small paper plate to the top of the larger paper plate so the outside "ridges" of each plate overlap.
5. Cut a circle out of black construction paper for an eye.
6. Glue the eye to the larger plate, near the small plate.
7. Glue black feathers to the large plate for wings.
8. Staple a few strips of tissue paper or streamers in different lengths in the fold of the large plate to make a tail.
9. Punch a hole in the large plate and tie a piece of yarn in a loop so that the toucan can hang or "fly."

Watch this craft "fly away" in "Two Talking Toucans," p. 18!

Frog

What You Need
Cardboard egg carton
Florescent paint
Paint brush
Glue
Hot glue gun
Scissors
Frog pattern (included on p. 59)
Green and red construction paper
Plastic "wiggly eyes"
Plastic bug

What You Do
1. Cut out two individual cups from the egg carton, making sure to cut them low enough so that when inverted, the entire rim can rest on a flat surface.
2. Using florescent paint, paint the outside of each cup. Allow these to dry.
3. Place a small line of hot glue along the inside of one wall of one cup.
4. Press the other cup to the line of glue firmly, leaving a small gap in the front. At this point, the cups should resemble a "V" shape (refer to picture).
5. Cut out pattern pieces and glue to egg carton.
6. Cut a tongue out of a piece of red construction paper and hot glue it to the inside of the opening.
7. Glue a plastic bug to the end of the tongue.

You can use your new frog on the songs "'Grr-umph!' Went the Little Green Frog," p. 28, "Ten Little Froggies," p. 30 and "Five Little Speckled Frogs," p. 38!

Binoculars

What You Need
Toilet paper tubes
Tempera paint
Paint brush
Hole punch
Hot glue gun
Shoestring or heavy yarn

What You Do
1. Glue two tubes together.
2. Paint the tubes.
3. Punch a hole on the outside of each tube.
4. String a long shoestring or piece of heavy yarn through the holes for hanging.

Safari Maps

What You Need
Large brown paper bag
Crayons or markers
Stamps
Stickers

What You Do
1. Tear the paper bag into large sections.
2. "Crumple" and "uncrumple" the paper several times until it becomes soft.
3. For very soft maps, rub the paper with vegetable shortening, crumple it into a ball and allow it to dry.
4. Lay treated paper out flat.
5. Use crayons or markers to draw a map to treasure, animals, waterfalls, etc.
6. Stickers and stamps can also be added for decoration.

Jungle Safari Vest

What You Need
Large brown paper grocery bag
Tempera paint or markers
Paint brush
Scissors

What You Do
1.   Cut out holes in the bag for arms and head.
2.   Use paint or markers to decorate with jungle colors and scenes.

Jungle Cards

What you need
Jungle Card cut-outs (included on p. 60-61)
Colored markers
Scissors
Felt
Glue

What You Do
1.   Copy or trace the cut-outs.
2.   Glue felt to the back of the page.
3.   Cut out the squares to make the cards.

Use the Jungle Cards for these fun songs!
"Going to the Jungle, Sing What We Should Bring," p. 12
"Walking in the Jungle, What Do You See?" p. 39

Tropical Fruit Tasting and Painting

What You Need
2-3 pieces each of assorted tropical fruits (star fruit, kiwi, papaya, coconut, etc)
Knife (for adult use ONLY!)
Paper plate
Tempera paint in different colors
Large pieces of construction paper

What You Do
1. Bring in several different tropical fruits, such as star fruit, mango, pineapple, etc.
2. Allow the children to observe the fruits and discuss similarities and differences.
3. Talk about the origins of each fruit with the class.
4. Cut up some pieces of fruit and allow the children to sample a taste.
5. Cut other fruits in half and place them on a paper plate covered with different colors of tempera paint.
6. Stamp the painted fruits onto construction paper to make a unique design.

Jungle Craft Patterns

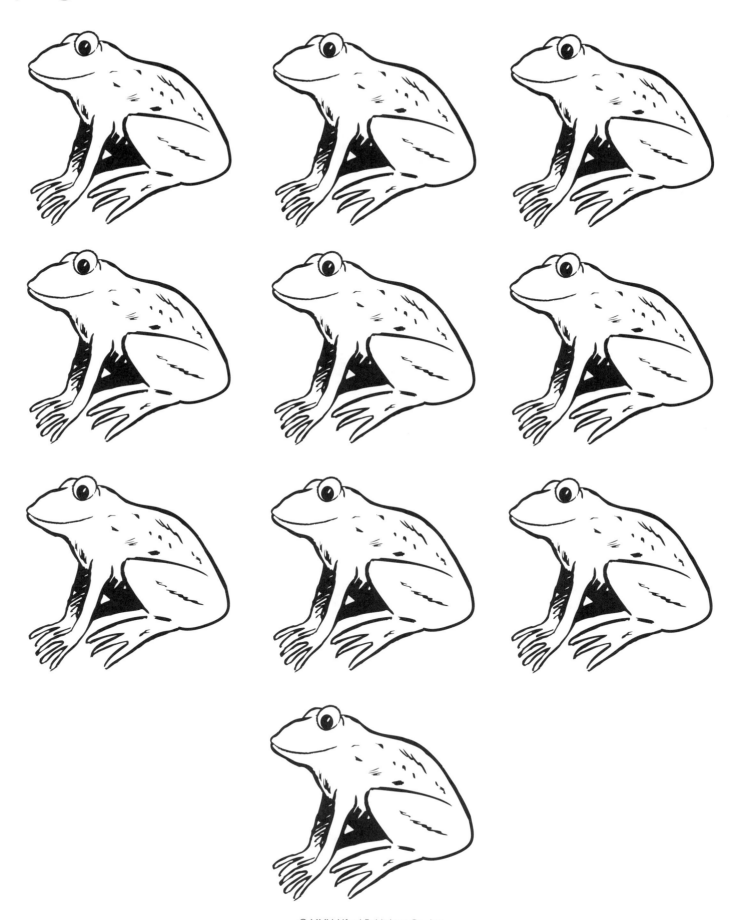

bat

parrot

monkey

butterfly

cheetah

cobra

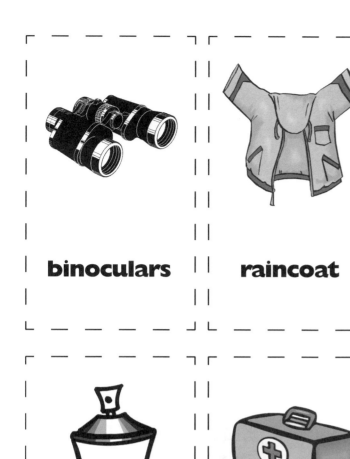

binoculars

raincoat

umbrella

camera

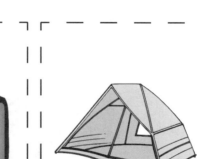

bug spray

first aid kit

tent

lunch

hiking boots

water bottle

hat

backpack

Jungle Room Décor

Small Jungle Trees

What You Need
Newspaper
Tape
Scissors
Green, brown, black and white tempera paint
Paint brushes

What You Do
1. Paint several sheets of newspaper in different shades of green paint (add white or black to change shade) and allow to dry.
2. Paint one sheet of paper in brown and allow to dry.
3. Overlap several sheets of green and roll into a tube.
4. Tape the bottom of the tube.
5. Make four to six 1" wide cuts from the end to about one-third of the way down the length of the tube.
6. Gently pull up on one of the inside "leaves" from the center.
7. Roll up the brown paper to make the tree trunk and attach to the leaves.
8. Add monkeys, birds, and snakes for effect!

Large Jungle Tree

What You Need
Brown butcher paper
Scissors
String
Stapler

What You Do
1. Using scissors, cut long lengths of butcher paper.
2. Twist the paper up to make branches.
3. Hang from ceiling using string.
4. Use butcher paper again, this time cutting lengthwise into fourths.
5. Twist again, and hang from branches to make vines.
6. Branches and vines can be stapled together to increase length.

Waterfall

What You Need

*Adults Only!

2 large round basins or 1 large plastic water bottle
Knife or jigsaw
Bricks or blocks
Roll of plastic
Water pump
1 large basin
Plastic, silk or live plants
Pebbles
Bark

What You Do

1. Using the knife or jigsaw, cut the water bottle in half, or use two basins.
2. Place one basin on the floor.
3. Use the bricks or blocks to create two different levels for the water bottles or basins.
4. Set up the water pump to pump the water from the lower level to the upper level.
5. Decorate with stuffed jungle animals, flowers, pebbles, fruits or previous crafts from this book.
6. Cover the floor with bark to complete the jungle illusion.

The *Jungle Beat* CD can also be played as part of the ambience of this craft!

Jungle Snacks

Tropical Fruit Salad

What You Need
Assorted tropical fruits (2-3 pieces of each): Star Fruit, Pineapple, Papaya, Banana, etc.
Bowls
Spoons

What You Do
1.   Cut up fruits and place in bowls with spoons.
2.   Have the children make their own tropical fruit salad by selecting fruits to put in their bowl.

Monkey Dogs

What You Need
Bananas
Peanut butter or strawberry jam
Hot dog bun
Plastic knife

What You Do
1.   Cut a banana in half lengthwise.
2.   Spread peanut butter or jam on the inside of a hot dog bun.
3.   Place the banana in the bun, close and enjoy!

Elephant Feet

What You Need
Round sugar cookies
White frosting
Black food coloring
Plastic knives
Gum drops or jellly beans

What You Do
1. Stir black food coloring into the frosting, until it is gray.
2. Using plastic knives, frost the cookies.
3. Use different colored gum drops or jelly beans for "polished" toes!

Gelatin Jungle Animals

What You Need
Gelatin snack mix
Animal cookie cutters
Cookie sheet
Mixing bowl
Paper plates to be decorated with the jungle gelatin animal

What You Do
1. Prepare the gelatin, using directions for a thicker mixture.
2. Pour onto a cookie sheet and refrigerate.
3. Use cookie cutters to cut out the animal shapes.
4. Use a spatula to transfer the gelatin animals to paper plates.
5. This craft can be used as an opportunity to observe the process of turning liquids to solids!

Snakeskin Sticks

What You Need

2 Bananas
1/2 c. Peanut butter
1 c. Puffed rice cereal
4 Wooden craft sticks

What You Do

1. Cut bananas in half crosswise.
2. Insert wooden craft stick into cut end, halfway into banana.
3. Spread peanut butter over banana.
4. Roll in rice cereal.

Pineapple Lions

What You Need

Paper plate
Spoon
Fork
Pineapple ring
Carrot
Grater (for adults ONLY!)
Cottage cheese or yogurt
Black or green olives
Thin pull-apart licorice

What You Do

1. CAREFULLY grate carrots.
2. Place pineapple ring on plate.
3. Fill in center of ring with cottage cheese or yogurt.
4. Put grated carrot around the ring to create the lion's mane.
5. Use the olives for eyes and licorice for the whiskers.

Cocoa Bean Chocolate Treats

What You Need
Cocoa beans
Coffee beans
Semi-sweet or milk chocolate chips or bars
Microwavable bowl
Pretzels

What You Do
1.   Allow children to taste, smell and touch cocoa and coffee beans.
2.   Talk about the origins of each bean with the class.
3.   Melt chocolate in microwave.
4.   Dip pretzels in the chocolate and enjoy!

Frozen Bananas

What You Need
Bananas
Wooden craft sticks
Semi-sweet or milk chocolate chips or bars
Microwavable bowl
Pretzels
Chopped nuts (optional; be careful of allergies)

What You Do
1.   Cut a banana in half crosswise
2.   Insert wooden craft stick into cut end, halfway into banana.
3.   Freeze for at least 1 hour.
4.   Melt chocolate in microwave.
5.   Dip bananas in melted chocolate.
6.   If desired, roll bananas in chopped nuts.

Jungle Trail Mix

What You Need
Tropical food items:
Nuts (optional; be careful of allergies)
Grated coconut
Chocolate
Dried pineapple, guava, etc.
Banana chips
Mixing bowl
Individual bowls or bags

What You Do
1. Mix all ingredients together and enjoy.
2. Allow children to make up their own unique mixtures!

Nuts About Bananas!

What You Need
Bananas
Peanuts (optional; be careful of allergies)
Sugar
Cinnamon
Mixing bowl

What You Do
1. Chop up peanuts (for allergies, cinnamon and sugar may be used alone).
2. Add cinnamon and sugar to nuts in a bowl.
3. Stir until evenly blended.
4. Dip banana into nut mixture and eat.

Index of Songs

CD Tracks Listing

1. Jungle Beat Chant (with drums)
2. Jungle Music
3. Jungle Beat Chant (with body percussion)
4. We're Going to the Jungle Today!
5. Sixty Inches of Rain
6. Create Your Own Thunderstorm
7. Going to the Jungle, Sing What We Should Bring
8. Jungle Beat
9. Five Little Monkeys
10. The Spider Kept on Spinning
11. Two Talking Toucans
12. Bats
13. I'm Being Swallowed by a Boa Constrictor
14. Silly Sam
15. Up So High
16. Now My Shaker's Up / Where Are You?
17. Jungle Beat Chant (with Orff instruments)
18. The Butterfly
19. "Grr-umph!" Went the Little Green Frog
20. Ten Little Froggies
21. A Salamander
22. Matilda the Gorilla
23. The Elephant
24. One Little Elephant
25. Five Little Speckled Frogs
26. Walking Through the Jungle, What Do You See?
27. Guantanamera
28. Mister Sun
29. The Lion Sleeps Tonight
30. Jungle Beat Chant (whispers)

Instrumental Versions

31. We're Going to the Jungle Today!
32. Sixty Inches of Rain
33. Jungle Beat
34. I'm Being Swallowed by a Boa Constrictor
35. "Grr-umph!" Went the Little Green Frog
36. Matilda the Gorilla
37. One Little Elephant
38. Five Little Speckled Frogs
39. The Lion Sleeps Tonight

The Instrumentalists / Vocalists
Ute Braun - Orff, accordion
Paul Cummings - Orff, vocals
Martin Espino - Orff, panpipes, guitar, "jungle percussion", vocals
Luc Kleiner - Orff, piano, drums, vocals
Lynn Kleiner - Orff, kalimba, piano, recorders, vocals
Cynthia Mendenhall - vocals
Jessica Tunick - vocals

The Young Vocalists
Jana Heckerman
Ellie Tsao Pearson
Acacia J. Peterson
James R. Peterson
John Plaster

Recorded at South West Sound, Sierra Madre, CA
Music arranged by Lynn Kleiner © 2006 Music Rhapsody
"The Lion Sleeps Tonight" arranged by Paul Cummings

About the Author

Lynn Kleiner began her "active" approach to music education in 1978. She is founder and director of Music Rhapsody, a music school for parents and infants, toddlers and young children up through the eighth grade. She and her team of teachers also provide music to day care centers, preschools and elementary schools. Lynn is a frequent presenter for organizations such as Music Educator's National Conference (MENC), the American Music Therapy Association, the American Orff Schulwerk Association (AOSA), and the Victorian Orff Association (Australia), as well as school districts, early childhood associations and parent groups worldwide.

Lynn is the author of *Kids Make Music*, Babies *Make Music Too!*, *In All Kinds of Weather, Kids Make Music!*, *The Sound Shape Play Book*, and *Kids Can Listen, Kids Can Move!* She also has her own line of percussion instruments through REMO, Inc. Lynn's instrument and video/DVD kits, known for their high quality and durability, have received the prestigious Oppenheim award, the Dove Award, and the recommendation of the National Parenting Association. Her DVD, *In All Kinds of Weather, Kids Make Music!*, was named one of *Parenting Magazine*'s video picks of the month.

To contact Music Rhapsody: 1-888-TRY-MUSIC or 310-376-8646 or go to **www.musicrhapsody.com**.

Notes:

Notes: